• Start TO Finish

Sports Gear

FROM
Plastic TO Soccer Ball

● ROBIN NELSON

 LERNER PUBLICATIONS COMPANY › Minneapolis

Copyright © 2015 by Lerner Publishing Group, Inc.

Lerner Publications Company
A division of Lerner Publishing Group, Inc.
241 First Avenue North
Minneapolis, MN 55401 USA

For reading levels and more information, look up this title at www.lernerbooks.com.

Library of Congress Cataloging-in-Publication Data

Cataloging-in-Publication Data for *From Plastic to Soccer Ball* is on file at the Library of Congress.
ISBN: 978-1-4677-3889-7 (LB)
ISBN: 978-1-4677-4743-1 (EB)

Manufactured in the United States of America
1 – CG – 7/15/14

TABLE OF Contents

I love playing soccer. How is a soccer ball made?

First, cloth is glued to the cover.

The outside cover of a soccer ball is made of **plastic**. The plastic keeps water from getting inside the ball. Up to four layers of cloth are glued to the plastic to make it strong. The layers help the ball keep its shape.

Next, a machine cuts the panels.

A machine cuts the cover into shaped pieces. The cutting machine also punches holes around the edges of each panel. These holes are for stitching the panels together.

The panels are printed.

A machine or a worker prints **logos** and other designs on the panels. A special fast-drying paint is used.

Then the panels are stitched together.

The soccer ball is put together inside out. Before the worker stitches the last panels, he or she turns the ball right side out. That way, the stitches can't be seen. It takes between one and three hours for a worker to stitch one soccer ball.

The bladder is made.

The bladder holds the air inside a soccer ball. Rubber is heated and put in a mold. The rubber forms a balloon. Then it cools.

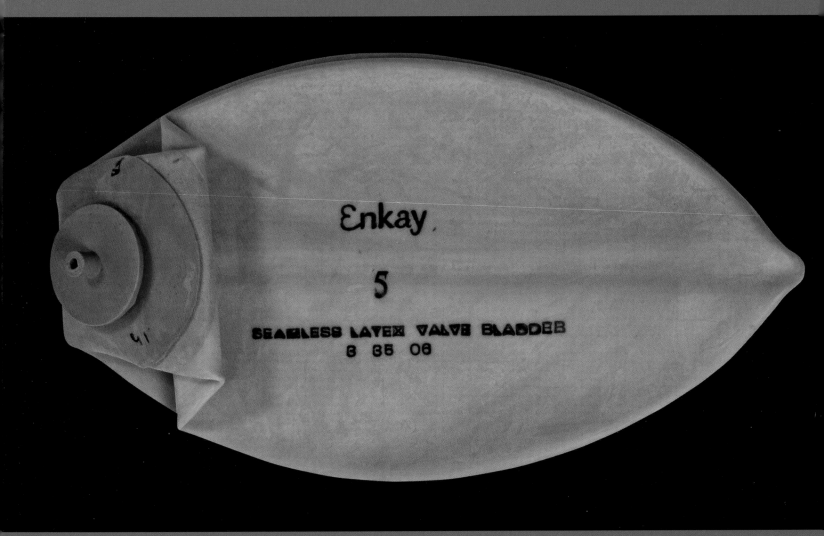

A valve is added to the bladder.

A valve is attached to the bladder. The valve lets air into the ball but keeps it from leaking out.

Next, a worker adds the bladder.

A worker tucks the bladder inside the cover. The valve is glued behind a small hole in the cover. Then the last panels are stitched together.

Air is pumped into the ball.

Air is pumped into the soccer ball through the valve. Air is added until the ball is round and firm. Then a worker checks the ball for air leaks. He or she makes sure it is the right size and weight.

Finally, the soccer ball is shipped.

The finished soccer ball is put in a box. Then it is sent to a store. The soccer ball is ready to kick!

Glossary

bladder: a balloon-like, air-filled bag inside a ball

cloth: material made by weaving threads together

logos: symbols used to identify a company

panels: pieces of material that are part of a larger surface

plastic: a light, strong substance that can easily be made into different shapes

valve: a device that controls the flow of air in and out of a ball

Further Information

Brown, Monica. *Pelé, King of Soccer/Pelé, El rey del fútbol.* New York: Rayo, 2009. Read the true life story—in English and Spanish—of Pelé, the first man in the history of soccer to score a thousand goals and become a legend.

The Life Cycle of a Soccer Ball
http://www.epa.gov/osw/education/pdfs/life-soccer.pdf
Learn everything you've ever wanted to know about a soccer ball and the game of soccer around the world.

Nelson, Robin. *Soccer Is Fun!* Minneapolis: Lerner Publications, 2014. Find out about soccer basics, including equipment, rules, and how to play the game.

Official Match Ball: 2010 World Cup
http://www.soccerballworld.com/Jabulani_2010.htm
Read and watch videos about the creation of the soccer balls used in the 2010 FIFA World Cup matches.

Wheeler, Lisa. *Dino-Soccer.* Minneapolis: Carolrhoda Picture Books, 2009. See what happens when a group of dinosaurs get together for a friendly game of soccer.

Index

Photo Acknowledgments

The images in this book are used with the permission of:
© Nicholas Burningham/iStock/Thinkstock, p. 3; © Aamir
Qureshi/AFP/Getty Images, p. 5; Romeo Gacad/AFP/
Getty Images/Newscom, p. 7; © Romeo Gacad/Getty
Images, p. 9, 17; AP Photo/K.M. Chaudary, p. 11; ©
Thorton Cohen/Alamy, p. 15; © Carl Payne/Alamy, p. 19;
© Patti McConville/Alamy, p. 21.

Front Cover: © In Green/Shutterstock.com

Main body text set in Arta Std Book 20/26.
Typeface provided by International Typeface Corp.